THE BEST SONGS OF JAZZ OF THE '60s AND BEYOND

Compiled and edited by Rob DuBoff

This series would not have been possible without encouragement from my family and friends. Thanks to: Grandma Lydia for helping me brainstorm for prospective titles, Mark Vinci and Mark Davis for sparking my interest in song collection, Jim and Jane Hall for their enthusiasm, Noel Silverman for being my advocate, Doug and Wendy for giving me perspective, and especially my parents, Arlene and Andy, for their tremendous support, confidence and guidance.

Special gratitude to Heather for being my sounding board, problem solver, editor, frequently-more-accurate extra set of ears and most importantly, my best friend. Without your unconditional support this project would not be.

THE JAZZ BIBLE™ and JAZZLINES PUBLICATIONS™ are trademarks used under license from Hero Enterprises, Inc.
Compiled and edited by Rob DuBoff for Jazzlines Publications™, a division of Hero Enterprises, Inc.

ISBN 0-7935-5809-3

7777 W. BLUEMOUND RD. P.O. BOX 13819 MILWAUKEE, WI 53213

For all works contained herein:
Unauthorized copying, arranging, adapting, recording or public performance is an infringement of copyright.
Infringers are liable under the law.

Visit Hal Leonard Online at
www.halleonard.com

THE BEST SONGS FROM JAZZ OF THE '60s AND BEYOND

CONTENTS

- 9 ADAM'S APPLE
- 10 ALFIE
- 11 ALL ACROSS THE CITY
- 12 ALL BLUES
- 13 ALL I NEED IS THE GIRL
- 14 ALL TOO SOON
- 15 AND I LOVE HER
- 16 AS LONG AS HE NEEDS ME
- 17 AT LONG LAST LOVE
- 18 AT THE MAMBO INN
- 19 BERNIE'S TUNE
- 20 BETTER LUCK NEXT TIME
- 22 BLACK COFFEE
- 21 BLOOD COUNT
- 24 BLUE CHAMPAGNE
- 25 BLUE HAZE
- 26 BLUE IN GREEN
- 27 BLUE TRAIN (Blue Trane)
- 28 BONITA
- 30 BORN TOO LATE
- 29 BOYS AND GIRLS LIKE YOU AND ME
- 32 BROWN SKIN GAL IN THE CALICO GOWN
- 33 CALL ME IRRESPONSIBLE
- 34 CAST YOUR FATE TO THE WIND
- 36 CENTRAL PARK WEST
- 37 CEORA
- 38 A CHILD IS BORN
- 40 CHIM CHIM CHER-EE
- 39 CIRCLE
- 42 CIRCLE IN THE ROUND
- 43 COME BACK TO ME
- 44 COMES LOVE
- 45 A COTTAGE FOR SALE
- 46 COTTON TAIL
- 47 COUNTDOWN
- 48 COUSIN MARY
- 49 CRESCENT
- 50 DIDN'T WE
- 52 DINDI
- 54 DON'T RAIN ON MY PARADE
- 56 DREAM DANCING
- 51 ECAROH
- 58 EIGHTY ONE
- 59 EL GAUCHO
- 60 EQUINOX
- 61 E.S.P.
- 62 ESTRADA BRANCA (This Happy Madness)
- 63 FALL
- 64 FEE-FI-FO-FUM
- 66 A FELICIDADE
- 65 A FLOWER IS A LOVESOME THING
- 68 FOLLOW YOUR HEART
- 69 FOOTPRINTS
- 70 FOUR
- 71 FOUR ON SIX
- 72 FRAN DANCE
- 73 THE FRIM FRAM SAUCE
- 74 GEORGIA ON MY MIND
- 75 GET OUT OF TOWN
- 76 GIANT STEPS
- 77 THE GOOD LIFE
- 78 GOODNIGHT, MY SOMEONE
- 80 GREEN HAZE
- 81 HEAT WAVE
- 82 HOW CAN YOU FACE ME
- 83 HOW'DJA LIKE TO LOVE ME
- 84 I BELIEVE IN YOU
- 86 I GOTTA HAVE MY BABY BACK
- 87 I LEFT MY HEART IN SAN FRANCISCO
- 88 I LOVED YOU ONCE IN SILENCE
- 90 I REMEMBER IT WELL
- 91 I WAITED FOR YOU
- 92 I'D DO ANYTHING
- 93 I'LL ALWAYS BE IN LOVE WITH YOU
- 94 I'LL CLOSE MY EYES
- 95 I'LL FOLLOW YOU
- 96 I'LL KEEP LOVING YOU
- 97 I'LL KNOW
- 98 I'M ALL SMILES
- 100 I'M GONNA GO FISHIN'
- 102 IF EVER I WOULD LEAVE YOU
- 101 IF HE WALKED INTO MY LIFE
- 104 IF I RULED THE WORLD
- 106 IF YOU NEVER COME TO ME (Inutil Paisagem)

107 IMAGINE MY FRUSTRATION	168 ST. THOMAS
108 IMPRESSIONS	170 SHE (HE) TOUCHED ME
109 IN A MELLOW TONE	172 SIDEWINDER
110 INFANT EYES	173 SING ME A SWING SONG AND LET ME DANCE
111 IRIS	174 THE SINGLE PETAL OF A ROSE
112 JUDY	176 SLIGHTLY OUT OF TUNE (Desafinado)
113 JUJU	178 SO NEAR AND YET SO FAR
114 JUNE NIGHT	179 SOLAR
115 KILLER JOE	180 SOMEONE TO LIGHT UP MY LIFE (Se Todos Fossem Iguais a Voce)
116 LADY DAY	181 SOMETHING TELLS ME
117 LAZY	169 SONG OF THE JET (Samba Do Aviao)
118 LEGALIZE MY NAME	182 SOOTHSAYER
120 LESTER LEFT TOWN	183 SOUL MATES
121 LET THERE BE LOVE	184 SPEAK NO EVIL
122 LIKE A STRAW IN THE WIND	186 SPRING CAN REALLY HANG YOU UP THE MOST
123 LITTLE MELONAE	185 SPRING WILL BE A LITTLE LATE THIS YEAR
124 LITTLE OLD LADY	188 SUMMER'S OVER
125 LONELY HOUSE	189 A TASTE OF HONEY
126 THE LOOK OF LOVE	190 THAT LOOK YOU WEAR (Este Seu Olhar)
128 LOTUS BLOSSOM	191 THAT SUNDAY THAT SUMMER (If I Had to Choose)
127 LOVING YOU	192 THEN YOU'VE NEVER BEEN BLUE
130 MAKE SOMEONE HAPPY	194 THIS IS ALL I ASK (Beautiful Girls Walk a Little Slower)
131 MISSION: IMPOSSIBLE THEME	196 THIS MASQUERADE
132 MR. P.C.	193 TRISTE
133 MOMENT'S NOTICE	198 TUNE UP
134 MOON RIVER	199 TURN OUT THE STARS
135 MORE (Ti Guardero' Nel Cuore)	200 UNIT SEVEN
136 THE MUSIC THAT MAKES ME DANCE	202 UP JUMPED SPRING
137 MY BUDDY	201 VAGABOND DREAMS
138 MY FATE IS IN YOUR HANDS	204 VIRGO
139 MY FAVORITE THINGS	205 VIVO SONHANDO (Dreamer)
140 MY FOOLISH HEART	206 WAGON WHEELS
141 MY HEART AND I DECIDED	208 WALTZ FOR DEBBY
142 NAIMA (Niema)	210 WAVE
143 NEFERTITI	207 WEST COAST BLUES
144 NEVER WILL I MARRY	212 WHAT A WONDERFUL WORLD
146 NICA'S DREAM	213 WHAT AM I HERE FOR?
148 NIGHT DREAMER	214 WHAT KIND OF FOOL AM I?
149 O GRANDE AMOR	215 WHEN JOANNA LOVED ME
150 ON A CLEAR DAY (You Can See Forever)	216 WHERE FLAMINGOS FLY
151 ONCE I LOVED (Amor em Paz) (Love in Peace)	218 WHILE WE'RE YOUNG
152 ONCE IN A LIFETIME	217 WHISPER NOT
153 OPUS DE FOCUS	220 WHO CAN I TURN TO (When Nobody Needs Me)
154 THE PARTY'S OVER	222 WHO WILL BUY?
155 PASS ME BY	221 WHY DID I CHOOSE YOU?
156 PASSION FLOWER	224 WITCH HUNT
158 PEEL ME A GRAPE	226 WIVES AND LOVERS (Hey, Little Girl)
157 PENT UP HOUSE	225 WOULD YOU LIKE TO TAKE A WALK (Sump'n Good'll Come from That)
160 PEOPLE	228 YES AND NO
162 PINOCCHIO	229 YOU BETTER GO NOW
163 PRINCE OF DARKNESS	230 YOU'D BETTER LOVE ME
164 PURE IMAGINATION	231 ZINGARO (Retrato em Branco e Preto)
165 QUIET NOW	
166 RE: PERSON I KNEW	
167 SACK OF WOE	

FOREWORD

There are many publications called "fake books" in the music marketplace today. A fake book provides a collection of many standard and popular songs that are, in many cases, difficult to obtain. Unfortunately, fake books often utilize simplified or incorrect harmonies. When we are dealing with the music of many publishers over a period of a century, we often run into various differences in chord naming, notation and general editorial policy. Simply stated, many songs have come down to us with incorrect harmony and antiquated rhythmic notation. Often composers were consulted when their songs were prepared for sheet music editions, and a few even wrote their own piano/vocal arrangements for publication. But many established composers did not; so, many songs have been continuously available in arrangements that are not properly representative.

The idea of the 'standard classic song' is a relatively new one in American music. It was Frank Sinatra who popularized the performance of songs that were not current hit parade material, and even recorded them in 78 (and later 33 1/3) albums. In turn, jazz musicians and singers learned and collected the classic songs of Kern, Gershwin, Rodgers and Porter. Much of this repertoire was learned from recordings. The songs were often harmonically recomposed to make them more interesting for improvisation. In recent years, students seeking to learn these standards have similarly transcribed their favorite recordings. We felt that there should be a series of volumes containing the greatest popular songs with accurate melodies, chord progressions and lyrics. The Jazz Bible™ Series is the result.

Once the master title list was completed, the job of locating sources for each of the songs began. This proved to be a more complicated task than was first imagined. Songs were found in numerous libraries, such as The Library of Congress, The Smithsonian Archives, The Library of the Performing Arts at Lincoln Center, and many private collections throughout the United States. A number of these songs were quite rare, and some had to be assembled from scores or sketches. We then began listening to key recordings of these songs, with particular attention to classic jazz performances. (It was quite interesting to witness the metamorphosis of a song over many years of performances.) Through this research, we compiled the most commonly used chords for each song, many of which differed dramatically from the original sources. We refer to these substitute chords as the *adopted chord changes*. One of the difficulties in transcribing chord changes is distinguishing between harmonies that are commonly played and those that have been specifically arranged for a recording. To this end we have compared the adopted chord changes to the originals to ensure harmonic accuracy.

We have insured that this book be user-friendly by developing the following layout:

Generally, only one song is printed per page
A four-bar-to-a-line format has been used whenever possible
The form of each song can be seen at a glance with section marks that can also double as rehearsal letters

CHORDS

There were many cases where we felt it was appropriate to include both the original and the adopted set of chords. The adopted chords appear in italics above the original chords. Where only italicized chords appear in any measure or an italicized chord with no other chord underneath, the original music had the previous chord continuing. In some cases the adopted chords clash with the melody; these instances are noted. We have also included turnaround chords at the end of every song; these are always italicized. A chord with the suffix *alt* implies that any altered chord can be substituted. (Please see the chord glossary for possible altered chords.)

FORM

The form of most songs is clearly outlined with the use of section marks, each musically distinct section labeled a different letter. Where there is a section that is a variation of a preceding one, we have labeled the varying section with a superscript number. For example, A A^1 B A^2 would indicate that the form is A A B A with the second A varying slightly from the first A and the last A another variation. In cases where the verse to a song has been included, it is labeled V; an introduction is labeled I.

Naturally, each tune is open to difference in interpretation, and one should never rely solely on one source (be it printed or recorded) for learning songs. There is absolutely no substitute for developing one's ear through harmonic and melodic ear training, playing with others and listening to recordings.

Much research and thought went into the creation of this series, insuring that these fakebooks set new standards in printed music. They were undertaken with one thought in mind: you, the musician, should have the best possible printed sources for the finest songs of this century. I feel privileged to have been given the opportunity to work on this project. Thanks to Jim and Jane Hall, Noel Silverman, John Cerullo, Keith Mardak, and especially, Jeff Sultanof.

Please note that this is a **legal** fake book; **all fake books that do not display song copyright and ownership information somewhere on each title page are illegal.** Such publications violate U.S. intellectual property law by not reimbursing copyright owners for the use of their songs. Please help stop such infringements; do not buy these publications.

Rhythm Changes

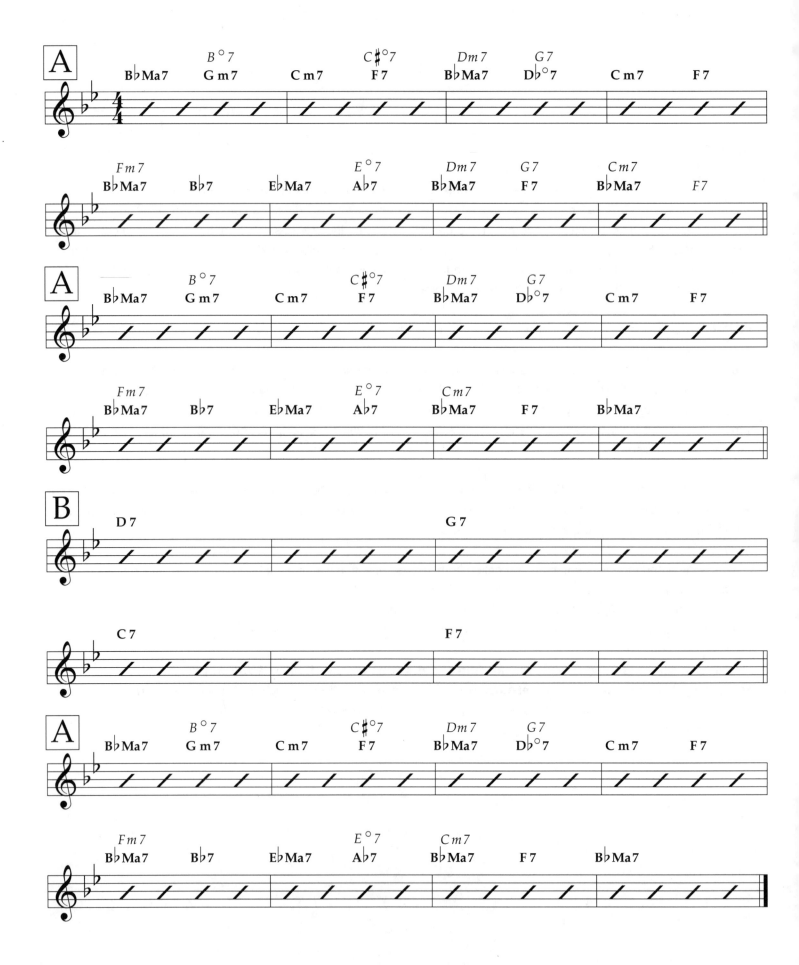

Blues Changes

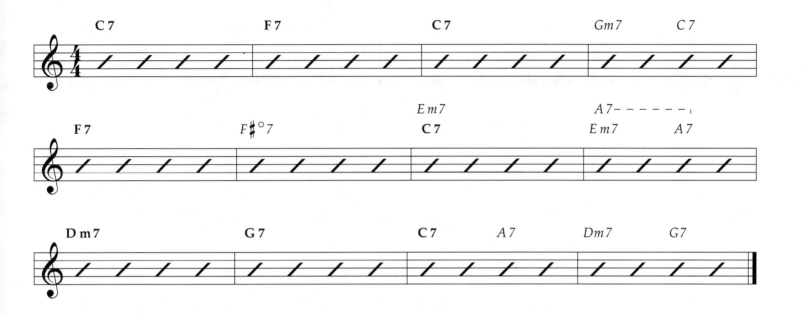

Minor Blues Changes

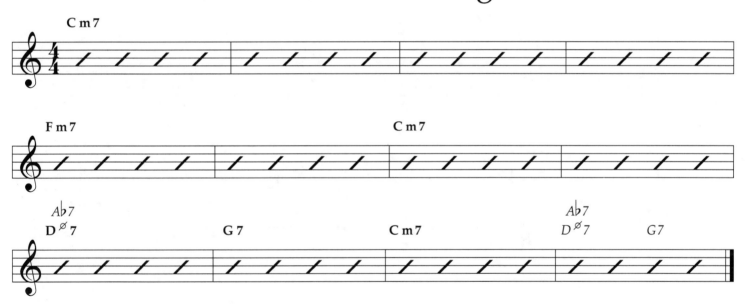

Chord Glossary

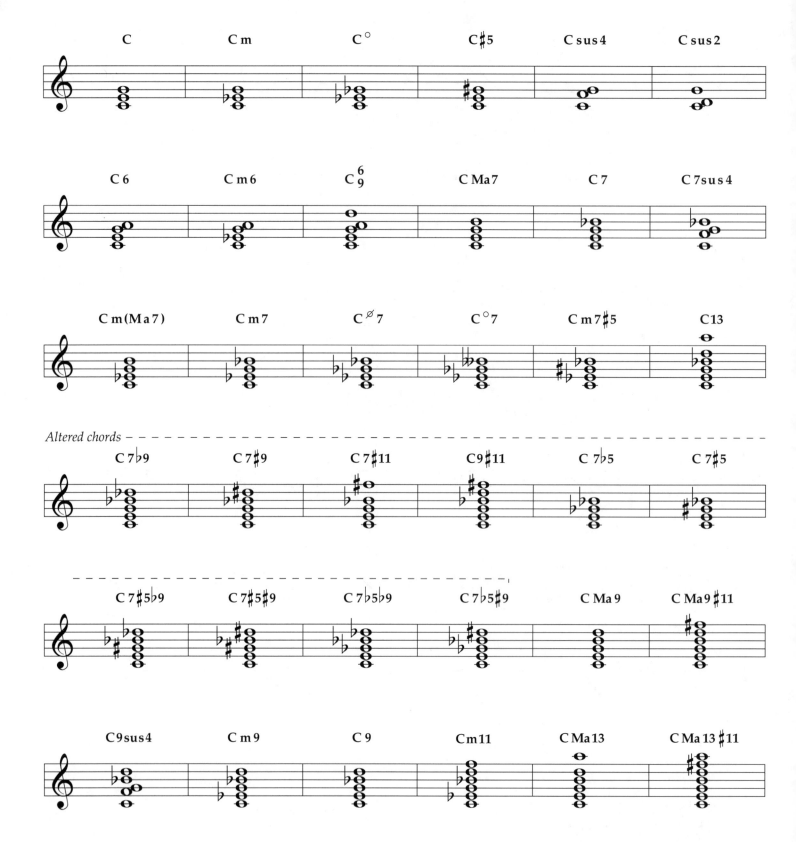

Adam's Apple

Medium

By Wayne Shorter

All Across the City

* Note: Use italicized chords first time only.

Copyright © 1964 Janhall Music
Copyright Renewed 1992
International Copyright Secured   All Rights Reserved

All Blues

By Miles Davis

All Too Soon

Ballad

Words and Music by Duke Ellington and Carl Sigman

Blood Count

Blue Haze

Medium

By Miles Davis

Blue in Green

By Miles Davis

Ballad

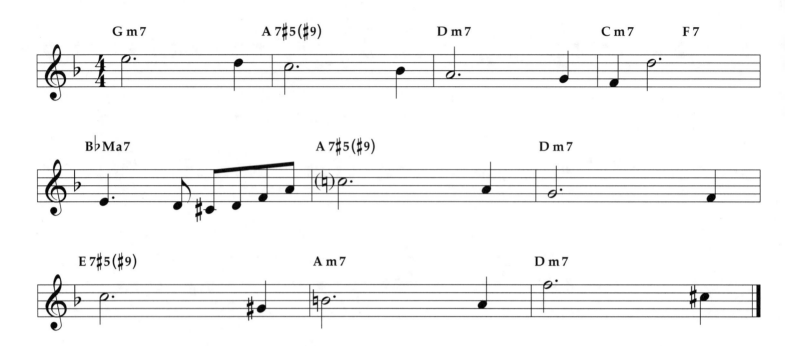

Blue Train
(Blue Trane)

Medium

By John Coltrane

Note: For solos, use standard blues changes in E flat (See "Blues Changes").

Copyright © 1957 (Renewed 1985) JOWCOL MUSIC
International Copyright Secured   All Rights Reserved

Bonita

Born Too Late

Call Me Irresponsible

from the Paramount Picture PAPA'S DELICATE CONDITION

Words by Sammy Cahn
Music by James Van Heusen

Cast Your Fate to the Wind

Central Park West

By John Coltrane

Ballad

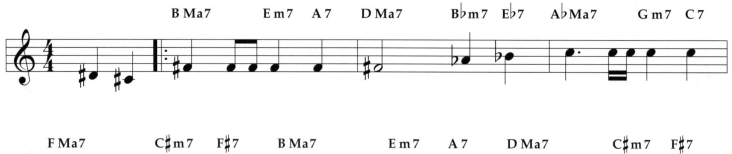

Copyright © 1977 JOWCOL MUSIC
International Copyright Secured   All Rights Reserved

A Child Is Born

Circle

Ballad

By Miles Davis

Circle in the Round

Medium

By Miles Davis

A Cottage for Sale

Ballad

Words by Larry Conley
Music by Willard Robison

Copyright © 1930 by DeSylva, Brown & Henderson, Inc.
Copyright Renewed, Assigned to Chappell & Co.
International Copyright Secured   All Rights Reserved

Cotton Tail — By Duke Ellington

Note: For solos, use standard rhythm changes in B flat (see "Rhythm Changes").

Countdown

By John Coltrane

Cousin Mary

By John Coltrane

Copyright © 1974 (Renewed 2002) JOWCOL MUSIC
International Copyright Secured   All Rights Reserved

Crescent

Slowly

By John Coltrane

Ecaroh

Medium

By Horace Silver

Dindi

Medium Bossa Nova

Music by Antonio Carlos Jobim
Portuguese Lyrics by Aloysio de Oliveira
English Lyrics by Ray Gilbert

Don't Rain on My Parade
from FUNNY GIRL

Words by Bob Merrill
Music by Jule Styne

Medium

A

Don't tell me not to fly, I've simply got to. If some-one takes a spill, it's me and not you.

Don't bring a-round a cloud to rain on my pa-rade.

A

Don't tell me not to live, just sit and put-ter. Life's can-dy and the sun's a ball of but-ter.

Who told you you're al-lowed to rain on my pa-rade? I'll march my

B

band out, I'll beat my drum. And if I'm

fanned out Your turn at bat, sir, at least I did-n't fake it.

Hat, sir, I guess I did-n't make it!

A

But wheth-er I'm the rose of sheer per-fec-tion or freck-les on the nose of life's com-plex-ion,

Copyright © 1963 by Chappell & Co.
Copyright Renewed
International Copyright Secured   All Rights Reserved

Dream Dancing

Eighty One

Medium

By Miles Davis and Ronald Carter

El Gaucho

By Wayne Shorter

Medium Latin

Equinox

Medium

By John Coltrane

E.S.P.

By Wayne Shorter

Fall

Medium Ballad

By Wayne Shorter

Copyright © 1968 MIYAKO MUSIC
Copyright Renewed
All Rights Administered by IRVING MUSIC, INC.
All Rights Reserved   Used by Permission

Fee-Fi-Fo-Fum

Medium

By Wayne Shorter

A Felicidade

Footprints

By Wayne Shorter

Medium

Four

Bright — By Miles Davis

Copyright © 1963 Prestige Music
Copyright Renewed
International Copyright Secured   All Rights Reserved

Four on Six

Medium

By John L. "Wes" Montgomery

Fran Dance

By Miles Davis

Medium

The Frim Fram Sauce

Giant Steps

By John Coltrane

Fast

Green Haze

Ballad

By Miles Davis

I Believe in You
from HOW TO SUCCEED IN BUSINESS WITHOUT REALLY TRYING

Medium

By Frank Loesser

I Gotta Have My Baby Back

I'll Always Be in Love with You

Medium

Words and Music by Bud Green, Herman Ruby and Sam H. Stept

Note: This song is also played in 4/4 time.

Copyright © 1929 Shapiro, Bernstein & Co. Inc., New York
Copyright Renewed
International Copyright Secured   All Rights Reserved
Used by Permission

I'll Close My Eyes

I'll Keep Loving You

By Bud Powell

I'll Know
from GUYS AND DOLLS

Medium

By Frank Loesser

Impressions

Fast

By John Coltrane

Infant Eyes

Iris

By Wayne Shorter

Medium

Juju

By Wayne Shorter

June Night

Medium

Words by Cliff Friend
Music by Abel Baer

Just give me a June night, the moon-light and you. In my arms with all your charms 'neath stars a-bove, and we'll make love. I'll hold you, en-fold you, then dreams will come true. So give me a June night, the moon-light and you.

Copyright © 1924 ABEL BAER MUSIC and EMI FEIST CATALOG INC.
Copyright Renewed
All Rights for ABEL BAER MUSIC Administered by THE SONGWRITERS GUILD OF AMERICA
International Copyright Secured   All Rights Reserved

Killer Joe

By Benny Golson

Copyright © 1959 (Renewed 1987) IBBOB MUSIC, INC. d/b/a TIME STEP MUSIC (ASCAP)
International Copyright Secured   All Rights Reserved

Lady Day

By Wayne Shorter

Legalize My Name

Lester Left Town

Medium

By Wayne Shorter

Little Melonae

By Jackie McLean

Loving You

Music by Gerry Mulligan
Words by Judy Holliday

Mission: Impossible Theme

from the Paramount Television Series MISSION: IMPOSSIBLE
from the Paramount Motion Picture MISSION: IMPOSSIBLE

Medium

By Lalo Schifrin

Copyright © 1966, 1967 (Renewed 1994, 1995) by Bruin Music Company
International Copyright Secured   All Rights Reserved

Mr. P.C.

By John Coltrane

Fast

Note: For solos, use standard minor blues changes in C minor (See "Minor Blues Changes").

Copyright © 1977 JOWCOL MUSIC
International Copyright Secured   All Rights Reserved

Moment's Notice

The Music That Makes Me Dance
from FUNNY GIRL

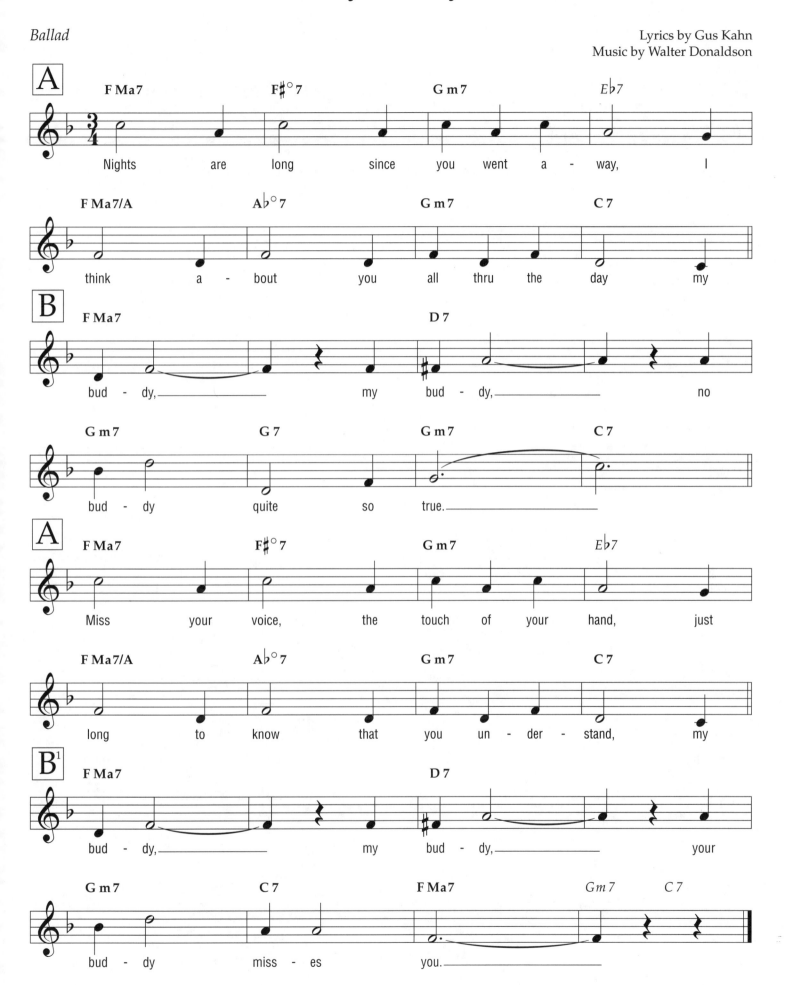

My Fate Is in Your Hands

Medium

Words by Andy Razaf
Music by Thomas "Fats" Waller

Copyright © 1929 by Chappell & Co. and Razaf Music, Inc.
Copyright Renewed
International Copyright Secured   All Rights Reserved

Nefertiti

Medium

By Wayne Shorter

Copyright © 1968 MIYAKO MUSIC
Copyright Renewed
All Rights Administered by IRVING MUSIC, INC.

144

Never Will I Marry
from GREENWILLOW

Medium

By Frank Loesser

Nica's Dream

Medium Bossa Nova   Composed by Horace Silver

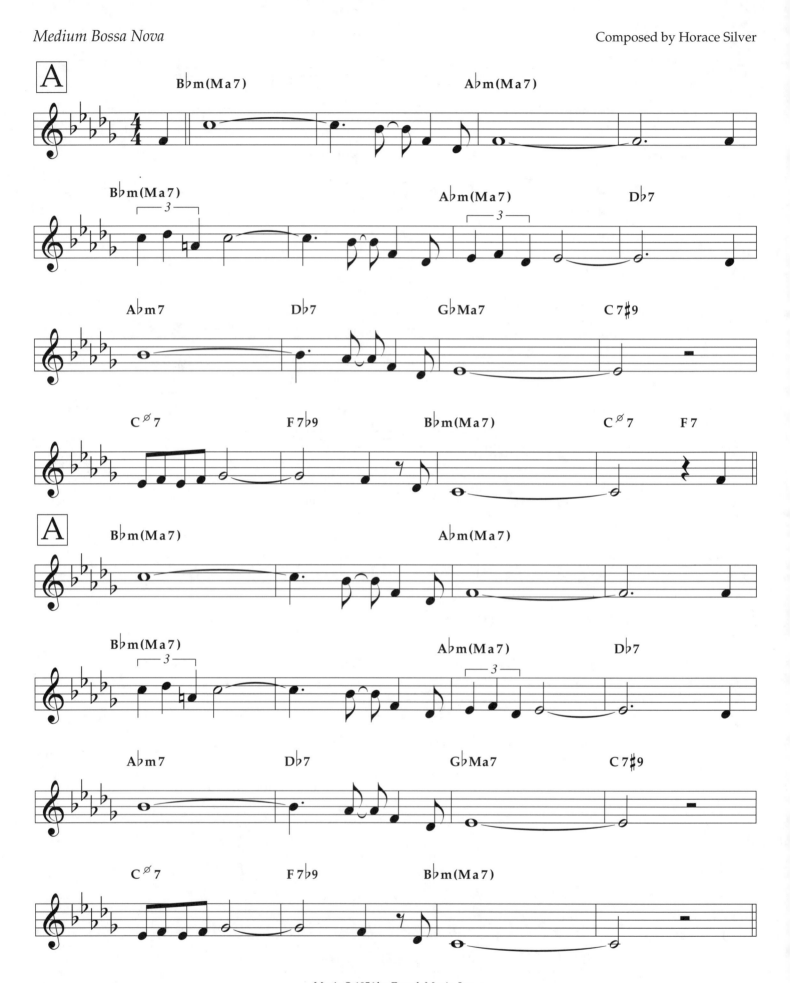

Night Dreamer

Medium

By Wayne Shorter

O Grande Amor

Once I Loved
(Amor em Paz)
(Love in Peace)

Opus De Focus

By J.J. Johnson

Medium

Passion Flower

Pent Up House

By Sonny Rollins

Peel Me a Grape

Pinocchio

By Wayne Shorter

Prince of Darkness

By Wayne Shorter

Quiet Now

Ballad

Music by Denny Zeitlin

Re: Person I Knew

Medium

Music by Bill Evans

Sack Of Woe

Medium Blues

By Julian Adderley

St. Thomas

By Sonny Rollins

Bright

Copyright © 1963 Prestige Music
Copyright Renewed
International Copyright Secured All Rights Reserved

Sidewinder

Medium

By Lee Morgan

The Single Petal of a Rose
from QUEEN'S SUITE

Ballad, freely

By Duke Ellington

Solar

By Miles Davis

Something Tells Me

Ballad — By Jane Hall

Soothsayer

Bright

By Wayne Shorter

Soul Mates

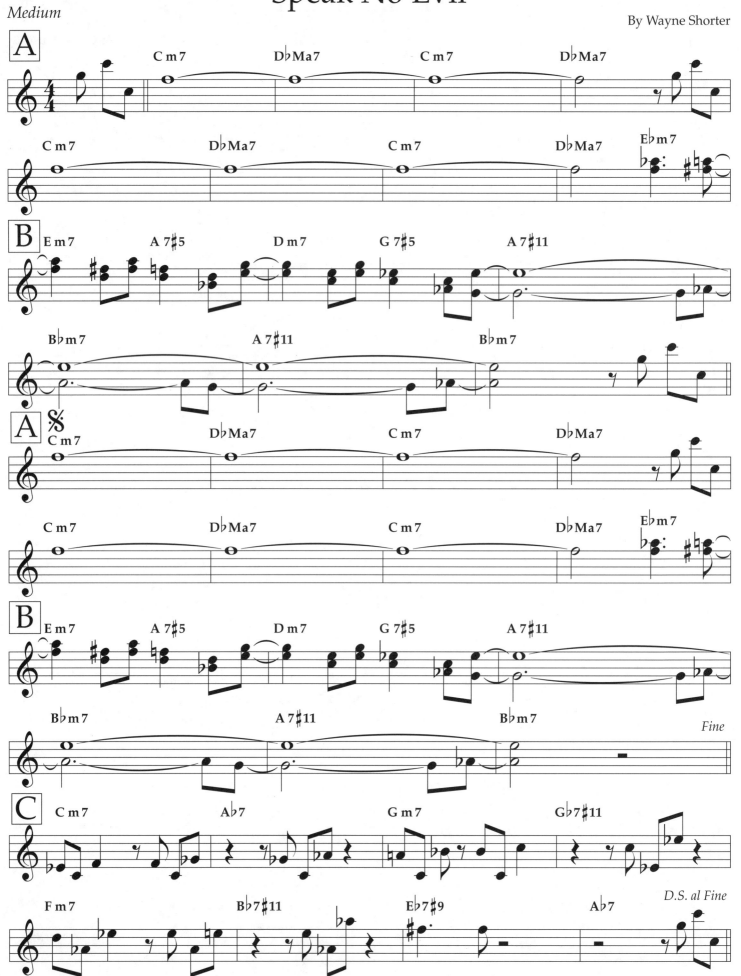

Triste

Medium Bossa Nova

By Antonio Carlos Jobim

A

| F Ma7 | | D♭Ma7 | |

Sad— is to live in sol - i - tude,—

| F Ma7 | A m7 | D 7♯5 |

far— from your tran - quil al - ti - tude.—

B

| G m7 | E⌀7 | A7 | D m7 | E 7♯9 |

Sad is to know— that no— one ev - er can live on a dream— that nev-

| A Ma7 | B m7 | E7 | A Ma7 | D7 | G m7 | C7 |

-er can be,— will nev-er be.— Dream-er a-wake,— wake— up and see,—

A¹

| F Ma7 | | F m7 | B♭7 |

your— beau - ty is an aer - o - plane,—

| F Ma7 | | C m7 | F7 |

so— high my heart can't bear— the strain.—

C

| B♭Ma7 | B♭m7 | A m7 | A♭°7 |

A heart that stops when you— pass by,— on - ly to cause me pain,—

| G m7 | C7 | F m7 | B♭7 | F m7 | B♭7 |

Sad— is to live in sol - i - tude.—

Copyright © 1967, 1968 Antonio Carlos Jobim
Copyright Renewed
Published by Corcovado Music Corp.
International Copyright Secured   All Rights Reserved

Tune Up

Bright

By Miles Davis

Turn Out the Stars

Unit Seven

Medium or Bright

By Sam Jones

Vagabond Dreams

Virgo

Ballad

By Wayne Shorter

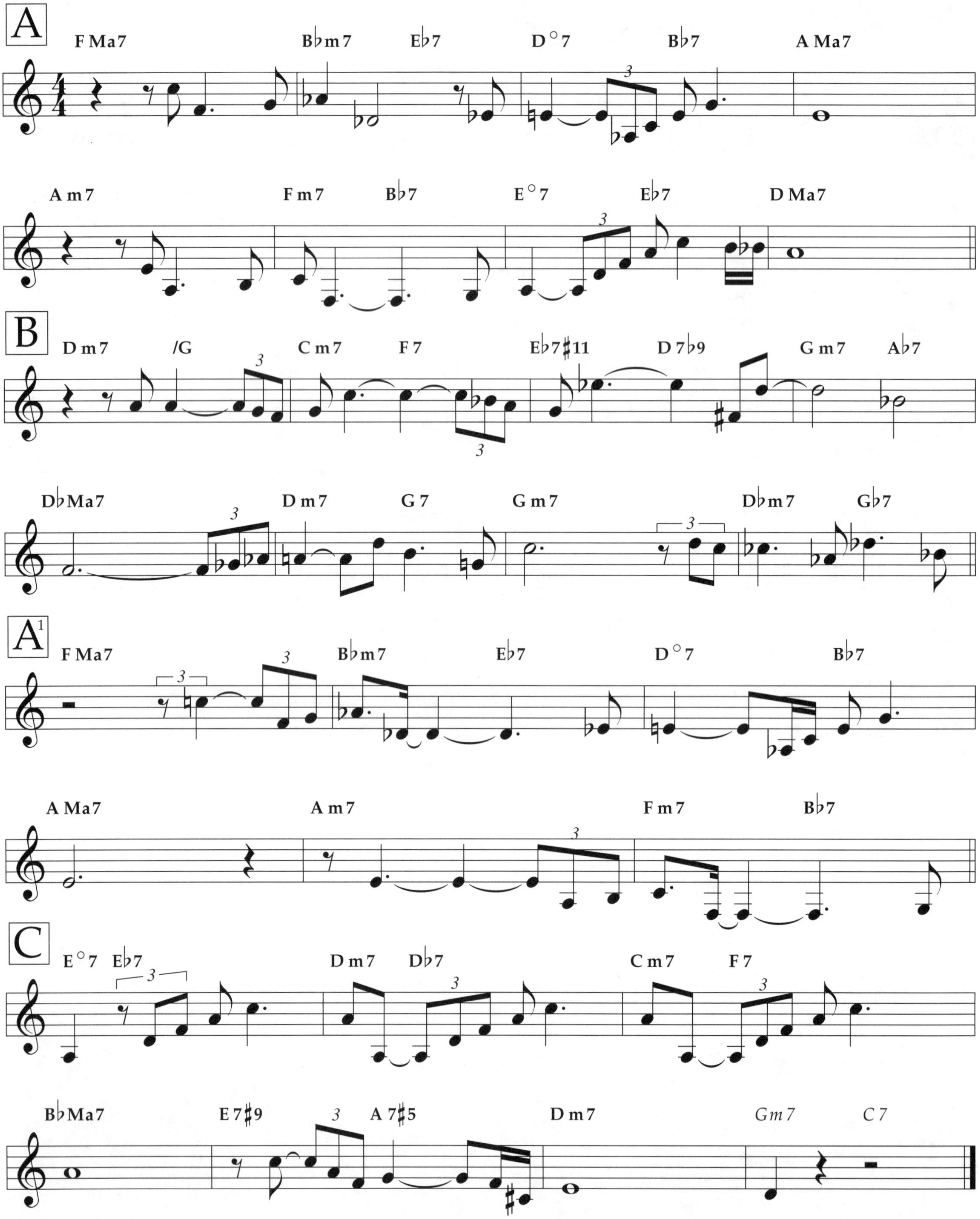

West Coast Blues

Medium

By John L. "Wes" Montgomery

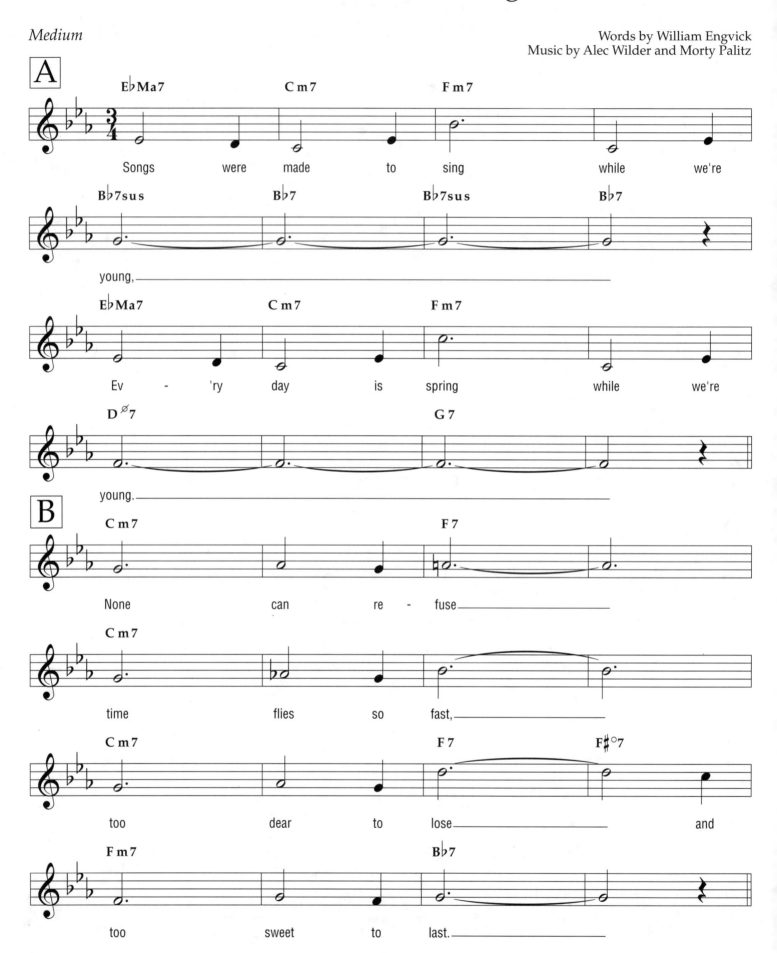

Witch Hunt

Fast   By Wayne Shorter

Yes and No

By Wayne Shorter

Zingaro
(Retrato em Branco e Preto)

Medium Bossa Nova

By Antonio Carlos Jobim

Copyright © 1965 Antonio Carlos Jobim
Copyright Renewed
Published by Corcovado Music Corp.
International Copyright Secured   All Rights Reserved

More Jazz Bibles

from **Hal•Leonard**

Each of the outstanding fake books in the *Jazz Bible* series features melody lines, lyrics and chords for 200 of the best jazz standards of all time. For piano, guitar, electronic keyboard and all C instruments.

RAGTIME & EARLY JAZZ – 1900-1935

Ain't Misbehavin' • All of Me • Autumn in New York • Basin Street Blues • Blue Skies • Body and Soul • Can't Help Lovin' Dat Man • Cocktails for Two • Everybody Loves My Baby • Falling in Love with Love • Gee Baby, Ain't I Good to You • Have You Met Miss Jones? • How Deep Is the Ocean • It Don't Mean a Thing (If It Ain't Got That Swing) • Just a Gigolo • Mood Indigo • Moonglow • My Blue Heaven • My Romance • Ol' Man River • Puttin' On the Ritz • Remember • Solitude • St. Louis Blues • When I Take My Sugar to Tea • When My Baby Smiles at Me • Why Was I Born? • You Made Me Love You • You Took Advantage of Me • You're My Everything • more!
00240074 ....$22.95

JAZZ OF THE '50S

Alice in Wonderland • Autumn Leaves • Beyond the Sea • But Beautiful • Born to Be Blue • Cry Me a River • A Day in the Life of a Fool • Do Nothin' Till You Hear from Me • Fly Me to the Moon • Freddie Freeloader • Good Moring Headache • Harlem Nocturne • Here's That Rainy Day • I Wanna Be Loved • I'm Late • If I Should Lose You • In Walked Bud • Lady Bird • Lazy Afternoon • Lost in the Stars • Misty • Mona Lisa • My One and Only Love • Old Devil Moon • Picnic • Satin Doll • Stella by Starlight • Stolen Moments • Tenderly • Unchained Melody • When Sunny Gets Blue • Young at Heart • many more!
00240077 ....$22.95

THE SWING ERA – 1936-1947

April in Paris • Between the Devil and the Deep Blue Sea • Bewitched • Candy • Caravan • Cherokee • Darn That Dream • A Fine Romance • Heart and Soul • I'll Be Seeing You • I'll Walk Alone • I've Got My Love to Keep Me Warm • It's Only a Paper Moon • Marie • Moonlight in Vermont • My Funny Valentine • The Nearness of You • Pennies from Heaven • Prelude to a Kiss • Sentimental Journey • Stompin' at the Savoy • Stormy Weather • A String of Pearls • Take the "A" Train • Tuxedo Junction • You'd Be So Nice to Come Home To • more!
00240073 ....$22.95

JAZZ OF THE '60S & BEYOND

Alfie • All Blues • As Long As He Needs Me • Bernie's Tune • Black Coffee • Blue Champagne • Blue in Green • Blue Train (Blue Trane) • Bonita • Call Me Irresponsible • Cast Your Fate to the Wind • A Child Is Born • Come Back to Me • Don't Rain on My Parade • Eleven • Follow Your Heart • Four on Six • Georgia on My Mind • Giant Steps • Goodnight, My Someone • Green Haze • I Left My Heart in San Francisco • I Loved You Once in Silence • If I Ruled the World • Iris • Judy • Lady Day • Lester Left Town • Moon River • More (Ti Guardero' Nel Cuore) • Peel Me a Grape • Slightly Out of Tune (Desafinado) • This Masquerade • Triste • Waltz for Debby • What Am I Here For? • and more.
00240078 ....$22.95

Prices, contents and availability subject to change without notice.

FOR MORE INFORMATION, SEE YOUR LOCAL MUSIC DEALER, OR WRITE TO:

HAL•LEONARD® CORPORATION
7777 W. BLUEMOUND RD. P.O. BOX 13819 MILWAUKEE, WI 53213

Complete song lists online at **www.halleonard.com**

Visit Hal Leonard Online at **www.halleonard.com**